$2

Outback Wisdom

Outback Wisdom

SARA LOOKS AT LIFE

SARA HENDERSON

MACMILLAN

Pan Macmillan Australia

First published 1995 in Macmillan by Pan Macmillan Australia Pty Limited
St Martins Tower, 31 Market Street, Sydney

Reprinted 1995, 1996, 1997, 1998

National Library of Australia
cataloguing-in-publication data:

Henderson, Sara, 1936– .
Outback wisdom

ISBN 0 7329 0821 3.

1. Country life – Australia – Anecdotes.
2. Country life – Australia – Humor. I. Title

994

Typeset in 13/16pt Cocktail by Midland Typesetters, Maryborough, Victoria
Printed in Australia by McPherson's Printing Group
Jacket photograph: Peter Johnson

Dedicated to my mum and dad

If the power of the written word can help just ONE individual to face their problems and make positive moves to a better life, this indeed is a truly wonderful thing.

Preface

Since writing the two *Strength* books I have been asked so many times by readers for permission to reproduce parts of the books for various reasons: to be used in a motivational seminar; to be part of an inspirational speech; to help in therapy for depressed people; or even to be made into a sign to hang in the workplace.

I am constantly amazed at the response I received from people. One man said to me the other day that he had gained more knowledge to help him in his business from reading the two books than from any business manual or book dealing with that subject. But I think the most asked question is, 'Where did you find the strength to keep going? How did you face such challenges and survive?'

I have thought about this quite a lot since

writing the books and I have come to the conclusion that it is 'attitude' that determines how you handle and survive life. My next question to myself was where did I get my 'attitude'? It didn't take long to work my way back through my life and come up with the answer.

My mum and dad gave me my attitude to life.

Mum did all the talking. When it came to advice, she gave very clear and definite guidelines and signposts to follow. Some of these remain with me to this day, such as her expression, *Treat every living thing on the face of this earth as you yourself would like to be treated*.

When I was a young child, whenever we were going somewhere and saw a crippled person Mum would make me say quietly, *There, but for the grace of God, go I*. Even to this day when I see someone less fortunate than myself I find myself thinking, *Thank you, God, for making me healthy*. It is a reflex action; I don't even have to think about it.

Another of Mum's favourites that has proven true throughout my life is this,

Life is a circle: eventually you end up back at the beginning. Eventually you will have to face yourself and your actions of past years. Eventually you will pass this way again, so make sure you do the right thing this first time so you will be glad to pass by the second time around.

Mum would tell me I was fortunate enough to be given a good family name and it was my duty not to do anything that would bring shame or dishonour on my family. As a result, dating became a nightmare: as I walked out the door Mum would say quietly, *Don't do anything you wouldn't want to read as headlines in tomorrow's paper.* Someone would suggest something at a party and I would picture the headlines immediately! Boy, didn't that little piece of motherly wisdom curtail my teenage activities!

If a job is worth doing it is worth doing to the very best of your ability, was a saying constantly quoted to me.

And *When in doubt, ask your conscience*, caused me hours of argument with myself as a young child, trying to convince my conscience that my scheme was OK when all the time, in the back of my mind, I knew the answer.

Poppa usually sat back and let Mum do all the talking; he had complete faith that she would guide me along the right path. But even in silence my dad gave out a loud message. I never heard him speak badly about anyone. He was upstanding, truthful, honourable and kind to all things. A very strong message, that could not be ignored, was transmitted by Poppa.

Of course I have to mention Charlie's influence in my life.

Smile, no matter how much you dislike the job you have to do . . . I have deep smile lines!

Always look for the best in people . . . sometimes hard to do, but always effective.

Take a problem and turn it into an asset . . . this has

proven to be very valuable over the years.

All these words of wisdom have helped me greatly over the years, so I thought I would jot them and a few more down in this little book of sayings. I hope they can in some way help you with everyday life – help you develop an attitude, give you food for thought.

But, most importantly, I hope they give you the desire to take life by the throat and shake the living daylights out of it. Take charge. Make positive moves. Defeat the challenges. Call the shots.

Good luck!

Sara Henderson
July, 1995

All the strength you need to achieve
anything is within *you*.
Don't wait for a light to appear at the end
of the tunnel. Stride down there ... and
light the bloody thing yourself!

Greet everyone with a cool mind, a warm heart, a bright smile, a helping hand ... or as many of the above as possible, each day ... and life will take care of itself.

There is no such thing as failure.
So eliminate the word from your
vocabulary! Look upon any experience
that did not work as part of life's learning
curve. Then go on with the knowledge
gained from that experience to improve
your performance.

*I*t is not the events in our lives that are
wholly significant, but more importantly
how we deal with these events,
that makes us who we are.

The generosity of your time
is the most valuable gift
you can give.

The greatest teacher in the world is
the past. For there are only 'x' amount
of scenarios in life, and if we look back
in history, we can see them played
out again and again and again.
Many times. Many ways.
Same results.

Treat anger like a good meal. Take your time and digest it slowly. Listen to good music for hours after, and then drift off to a good night's sleep. In the light of a new day look at your anger again. Then think carefully before you act ... or you could end up with severe indigestion.

Judge people by the colour of their soul
... not their skin.

Some of the most difficult words
in the world to say:
I was wrong.
I am sorry.
I will break that habit.
I did not tell the truth.
I will try and change my ways.
I ... love ... you.
But if we said them regularly, with
feeling, imagine what a wonderful world
it would be.

Only look to the past to gain knowledge
to help avoid mistakes in the future.

We can learn so much from animals.
They give very clear signals,
without saying a word.

Despite all the propaganda,
there is life after
30 ... and 40 ... and 50 ... and 58 ...
I'll keep you posted on the rest!

Some time between 551 and 479 B.C.
Confucius said: 'I have never come
across anyone who admires virtue as
much as he admires sexual attraction.'
It would seem that things haven't changed
much in the last few thousand years.

It seems that after you write a
book, people think you change.
I certainly don't feel any different,
but here are a few remarks made during
some of my book tours:
'I knew her when she was normal.'
'Well I knew her when she was
just a person.'
'Well *I* knew her when she was human.'
Marlee assures me I'm still all of the above!

Treat yourself like the most expensive
machine in the world. If you were given
a car worth millions, would you put
low grade fuel and cheap oil in it?
Not service it and leave it out in bad
weather? Let someone ruin the interior?
Let someone else drive it?
Of course you wouldn't.
You probably wouldn't let anyone breathe
on it, let alone touch it. You are worth
much more than any car, so give yourself
the care and attention you deserve.

If a business produced a major deficit every year, it would soon be *out* of business. If the government produces a deficit every year, it simply thinks up more taxes and raises them regularly.

Remember, whatever you do to people,
the air, animals, trees, and the earth, will
in turn be done to you. If it is done in
the name of money, just remember, all
the millions in the world cannot buy
happiness, friends, love, family
or one breath of fresh air.

The spoken word can never be taken back. The written word can be erased, burned, flushed down the toilet, changed. The spoken word lives forever in someone's memory, can never be recovered, is never forgotten, can haunt you for life, can cause generations of suffering. Choose the spoken word with care ... once it leaves your lips, it is too late.

We are constantly bombarded
with all the negatives of life.
Crime ... catastrophe ... misery.
Counterbalance these with the positives.
There are so many good people doing
good deeds, every day. Make a point
to find out about all the good
that is around you.

𝒯oo often we are dissatisfied with life,
wishing for this or wanting to change
that. But you can't really change the
past, only the future. The knowledge
you gain from your experiences, good
and bad, would not have been gained,
if you had not had the experiences.
You must experience to grow,
with growth comes knowledge
and with knowledge ... you change.

The lure of money does funny things to people ... that are not funny.

It is not what you say, but how you say it, that sometimes offends.

When I order spare parts by phone
the chap finishes the conversation with,
'No worries.'
I start worrying.

Face-lifts take away the expressions of
life that have taken years to earn.
Your face is what you have become
and reflects the true you. Actually,
I can think of a few people who
definitely need a face-lift,
to hide what they have become!

Walk through life quietly
and confidently.
Amid panic and confusion
show those around you that solutions
come from silence and peace.

Take life by the throat and shake the living daylights out of it. Enjoy every day of your life and work at making each day better than the one before. There is a beautiful and truly wonderful world waiting out there for you ... It's all up to you.

❧

Eliminate greed, hate, envy, jealousy, revenge, ego and excess from your life ...
What an unrealistic thought! And what
a dull and boring lot we would be.
What we must do is control these
emotions, so we rule them ...
that is realistic.

I read somewhere that writers receive
what they write from somewhere
'out there';
that they don't really create what they
write. I'm not sure what I think about this,
but I can only hope whoever or whatever
is transmitting to me does not break
the connection!

You can live in the middle of a densely populated city and feel desperately lonely. Yet you can be by yourself in the vast expanse of the outback and not feel alone.

If you find true love, you are in heaven
and paradise on earth.

Men's attitude towards women is in
the hands of women who raise the
boys who grow into men.
All women today –
be you a mother, grandmother, aunt,
great-aunt, sister, cousin, niece –
educate the men in your life to understand
women and to accept them as equals ...
nothing more ... nothing less.

℘e live in the world of instant.
You name it, you can get it in an instant.
Tea, coffee, bread, cakes, virtually every
food, painting by numbers,
instant lotto ...
Make sure you don't make your
whole life instant. Worthwhile things in
life take time. Take time to develop a solid
foundation for a life that will stand the
test of time.

Silence is so hard to achieve when faced with lies and hate. But it is the perfect expression of your contempt for other people's actions.

Always live your life with one more
dream to fulfill. No matter how many of
your dreams you have realised in the past,
always have a dream to go.
Because when you stop dreaming,
life becomes a mundane existence.

If you harbour hate, keep it to yourself,
but work on eliminating it from your life.
If you cannot achieve this,
build a mental wall around your hate
and slowly block it out of your life,
then live your life outside the wall.
Hate starved of daily infusions of
emotion, energy, and sunlight dies.
If you cannot conquer it,
make sure you take it with you.
Never bequeath hate to your loved ones
and the next generation.

There is always a subtle way
of getting a point across
with the minimum of stress and fuss.
When we first came to the outback
I had to cook on a wood-burning stove
and could never get the men to chop the
wood. Every day they would leave after
breakfast and I would find myself with
only a few pieces of wood to cook lunch.
One morning the men departed, leaving
me, as usual, with only a few pieces
of wood. They all arrived back for

lunch and eagerly sat down to eat ...
I silently placed their plates before them.
For a while they all repeatedly looked
at each other and back at their plates,
not knowing what to do.
Charlie finally said, 'This food isn't cooked.'
I had nicely arranged a slice of raw steak
and raw potatoes, pumpkin, beans
and carrots on each plate.
I replied, 'Yes, the food is raw because I
have no chopped firewood to cook with.'
I never again had an empty firewood box.

When someone is rude or insults you,
smile – not sweetly – just smile.
Combined with silence,
it is the best of all possible replies.

Women who break through the 'glass ceiling' have one of the greatest responsibilities in the world today. They are laying the ground rules for future power relationships between men and women. Very clear messages must be given that women are there to help make the team a better one. You hear some stories of women's childish behaviour that make you wonder how they ever reached a position of power in the first place. These women are a menace to other achieving women.

⁂

Stress ... we all know it so well.
I am often asked how I survived so
much stress for years on end. I believe
it all comes back to taking care of yourself
and constantly adjusting the control
gauges. When you have heavy demands
on you and stress levels go up, it is
important to adjust the controls by
cutting back on things like cigarettes, alcohol
and coffee and to eat good fresh food.
Continuous stress requires more controls
and adjustments. Along with the above,

sleep is very important as well as taking
regular breaks from the pressure – if only
by closing your eyes for ten minutes and
blocking out everything.
The best way to look at stress
is to imagine it as a twenty foot long
boa constrictor which can wind itself
around and slowly squeeze the life out
of you. But if you chop it into twelve inch
pieces, it cannot harm you.

Look at your life as a beautiful fabric
woven from wonderful rich colours and
fine cloth. Make a plan,
one that is full of obtainable goals for
a happy life. Read through the plan
daily so that it becomes a permanent
part of your thought process.
Be alert every day for any
opportunity to further the plan,
no matter how small.

᪐

Also make a list of your dreams. Whenever possible, weave your dreams into the fabric of your life. Remember, only you can weave the cloth. Many people can give suggestions of colour and design, but the ultimate product is in your hands alone.

We can't eliminate racism, greed and hate from the dictionary ... but we can eliminate them from our lives.

Leadership is like wind on a field
of long grass. A gentle, constant, coaxing
wind has the grass quietly bending and
swaying in the one direction. A gusty,
uncontrolled, violent wind has the whole
field in disorder.

*O*ptimists are the elixir of life. They constantly remind the pessimists that life really isn't as hopeless as they think. They are the extra ingredient that makes life bubble—and cause the effervescent bubbles of hope to explode out of the formula of life, creating new ideas, dreams ... and progress.

If you continuously face challenges,
one of two things can happen: You either
collapse under the strain, lose confidence
in your ability and walk away defeated—
perhaps to fight again later or to just
drift into a life of non-challenge.
Or you win a few impossibles and are
then encouraged to have a go at the next
impossible. So that before long, you find
the impossibles have become possible.

❧

The human race must stop worshipping
the almighty dollar.

Lethargy in thought, deeds ... in life in general, can lead to extinction.

✍

An overweight patient whinged to her doctor, 'Doctor, how can I lose weight?' The doctor replied, 'Shut your mouth.'

Always beware of people with extreme views. Extremists are usually the problem in any situation ... whether good or evil. There has never been a truer saying than: 'Moderation in all things.'

Your body doesn't lie. If you listen to it
carefully, it will tell you everything you
need to know to keep healthy.

You never achieve anything completely alone. If you look at any one of your achievements you will see that there was always someone or something there helping you to achieve your goal.

*J*udge a person's capability of
performance, not their level of performance.
If a person gives you their 100 per cent ...
you can't ask for any more.

*P*roblems are a major part of life.
Don't whinge about why you always have
problems. Rest assured, no matter what,
throughout your life you will always have
to deal with problems. So don't waste
time. Get on with the solving. Take it from
someone who has been there – the solving
gets easier as you go along.

Back in the early sixties the stockcamp
arrived back at our tin shed homestead
after being out mustering for weeks.
One young jackaroo came into the kitchen
and asked me for some crunchy treacle
(these were the days of dry damper and
treacle). I told him there was no such
thing as crunchy treacle, but he insisted
he'd had it out on the camp.

When the cook came in later that day,
I asked him about it. He replied, 'Well
someone left the lid off the treacle at
morning tea and by the time I found it, it
was full of bull ants and flies. Too many to
fish out, so I gave it a good stir and left it.
The blokes steered clear of it, but that
young 'un from the city sure hoed in.'

Never attempt to discuss, argue or
solve problems with someone who
has been drinking, or is under the
influence of drugs.

ॐ

$\mathcal{A}$rrogant, overbearing, aggressive
people are to be avoided at all costs. They
deteriorate your energy, cause a
breakdown in your body's harmony and
deplete the spirit. If everyone avoided them
... they would have to change in order
to be part of society.

If you have to work with someone
who upsets you, makes you angry,
or who you just can't stand, start a
competition with yourself. Try to find
something nice about the person
and just concentrate on that.
You will find it helps make the time
spent with them much easier.

I could write volumes about mothers, indeed there have been volumes already written. So I will just say ... the world needs mothers.

I could also write volumes about fathers,
indeed there have already been volumes
written. So I will just say ... the world
needs fathers.

Each New Year's Eve tear up the previous year's list of resolutions and don't worry if you haven't achieved any ... Then on New Year's Day stick the list back together and start again!

Try and make the feelings and actions
of Christmas part of everyday life.

Loneliness is a state of mind.

We must take the time to treat each
person we meet as a special individual –
not just part of the blurred mass
we rush past every day.

To speak convincingly of peace
one has to speak harshly.

*N*ever take your blessings for granted
. . . or you will be sure to lose them.

The written word can reach down
through the ages and touch millions
of people.

When you are up against a problem, try and eliminate all your personal feelings and emotions as the first step in the solving process and you will probably find you have eliminated the problem.

A true friend is a rare gem in the
jewel box of life.

Commonsense is the basis of true happiness.

Childbirth . . . the only thing in life
that is not exaggerated!

Women do not gossip . . . they network.

❧

*I*f there was life after death,
I know Charlie would have come back
to tell me about it . . . and what he was
doing to improve it!

Ability has no gender.

Approach all creatures on equal terms.
Be sincere and listen politely to every living
thing, humans, animals, creatures, nature ...
because if you listen carefully,
everything in this universe has
something important to say.
And you and the world will be better off
if you pause ... and listen.

Remember, no matter what impossible
task you set yourself,
the beginning is that first step.